Shelly Bean the Sports Queen

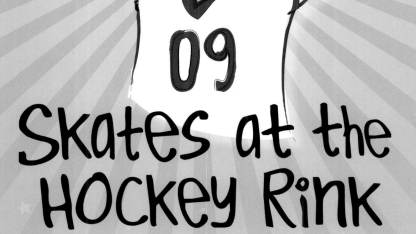

Skates at the HOCKEY Rink

By Shelly Boyum-Breen

Illustrated by Marieka Heinlen

DEDICATION: This book belongs to all young sports fans that love to play, work hard, try new things, and dream big. When I was six, I dreamed of playing in the NBA, NHL, NFL and MLB. I worked hard to make my dreams come true, and I made many friends and memories along the way. While I did not end up playing professional sports, I did do a lot of other cool things with my life—like write these books for kids! I am active every day and eager to share my passion for playing sports with others. My hope is that Shelly Bean inspires YOU to play.

ACKNOWLEDGEMENTS: A special thank-you to my youth coaches, parents, brothers, spouse, children, nephews and nieces and many friends who have supported me as I've grown as an athlete and as the creator of Shelly Bean the Sports Queen. Finally, an enormous thank you to the "backers" and Team Bean who worked creatively as a unit to help bring Shelly Bean to life.

For additional copies, visit
www.shellybeanthesportsqueen.com

PUBLISHED BY:
Level Field Press, LLC
2960 Everest Lane
Plymouth, MN 55447
shellybeanthesportsqueen.com

Illustrated By: Marieka Meinlen
Design & Print Production:
Blue Tricycle, Inc.

Boyum-Breen, Shelly.
    Shelly Bean the Sports Queen skates at the hockey
rink / by Shelly Boyum-Breen ; illustrated by Marieka
Heinlen.
    pages cm
    SUMMARY: Shelly Bean the Sports Queen learns about
friendship and team spirit while playing ice hockey.
    Audience: Grade 2.
    ISBN 978-1-4951-1493-9

    1. Hockey for girls--Juvenile fiction. 2. Team
sports--Juvenile fiction. [1. Hockey for girls--Fiction.
2. Sports for girls--Fiction. 3. Team sports--Fiction.
4. Friendship--Fiction.]   I. Heinlen, Marieka,
illustrator. II. Title.

PZ7.B6972Shs 2014   [E]
                   QBI14-600107

Team Shelly Bean

Shelly Bean loves to try new sports and she wants you to try new sports too! Let's see what she learns to play today. Then follow the tips at the end of the book and start playing with her!

Spike
co-mascot

Shelly Bean
the sports Queen

Buster
co-mascot

Ben
bigger brother

Matt
big brother

Maya
best buddy

Swoosh! Slam! Score! It was an exciting night. Shelly Bean and her family were watching the international women's ice hockey championship. Shelly sat too close to the TV. She swayed along with the colorful, racing skaters.

Sit back sweetie.

Shelly Bean felt her heart pumping fast—almost like she was on the ice herself. When their team won the gold medal, Shelly's family burst into cheers!

YES!!!!

I want to win a gold medal in hockey!

I bet you could Shelly Bean.

Shelly Bean loved sports, especially hockey. But before she had any hope of winning a championship, she decided that she should probably first learn how to … well … skate.

The next day, she dug through the hall closet and found her brother Ben's old hockey skates. Then, she dusted off his helmet. Now, she just needed someone to teach her how.

Ben helped his little sister pull the kneepads on over her winter clothes and they headed out into the cold, sunny day. Even their dog Spike, was ready for action!

Shelly Bean skipped eagerly down the street, pulling Ben by the hand behind her. On their way to the rink, they stopped at their friends' house to invite them along.

Ben helped Shelly Bean lace up her skates. Then he asked her to stand and wiggle her toes to make sure they weren't too tight. Finally, Shelly Bean put on her helmet and knew she was ready.

Out on the rink, Ben held Shelly Bean's hands tightly and pulled her across the ice on her skates.

As Shelly skated with her brother, she was surprised by how free she felt. But, it was harder than she thought!

Shelly could feel the blades of her skates wobble on the ice. She worried that maybe she looked as silly as she felt.

Shelly Bean! Are you wearing hockey skates?

Well, maybe not as silly as Spike. He had to worry about four legs, not just two!

Shelly tried to concentrate and ignore the people around her, but it wasn't easy. This gold medal business was going to be tougher than she thought.

But Shelly Bean was up for the challenge. She let go of Ben's hands and tried skating on her own. Her knees buckled and she waved her arms around in circles to try to keep her balance.

WHOa! WATCH Oooout Spike!

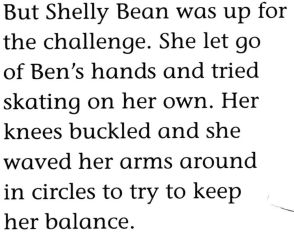

RuH-RoH!

Suddenly, she felt her feet slip out from under her, and SPLAT! Down she went on the cold, hard ice. Shelly felt the sting of bruises. She folded her arms across her chest and wanted to quit.

But before she could, Maya swiftly skated over to help Shelly Bean up. Pulling each other's hands, the girls started to laugh as they slipped and struggled to stand.

Just then, Carol, one of the hockey coaches, walked by carrying her team roster for the big game that night.

A smile slowly spread across Shelly's face. "People really believe in me," she thought.

Shelly Bean took a deep breath and wiped the snow off her clothes. She was ready to try again. Each time she tried, she was able to skate a little farther without falling down.

After a lot more practice with Ben, Maya, and Tait, Shelly Bean was able to skate across the rink without falling down. She even tried holding Ben's hockey stick. It felt amazing!

I'm so proud of you, Little Bean! You worked hard and kept trying... the qualities of a real champion!

Ben smiled to himself and thought, "Maybe she really will earn a medal in hockey someday."

As they all walked back to the warming house, Shelly Bean looked over her shoulder and saw Coach Carol helping players practice for the big game.

The big kids on the ice looked just like the gold medal champions on TV. Shelly Bean imagined herself growing up to be one of them someday.

Shelly Bean had convinced herself and a few others too, that hockey was going to be a lot of fun.

I'm sorry for making fun of you, Shelly Bean. Hockey looks like fun! Can we try it with you sometime?

As the kids warmed up, Shelly Bean took one last shot, Hey! Spike was a pretty good goalie!

23

When she got home, Shelly Bean changed out of her wet clothes and into her warm, fuzzy PJs. She did one of her famous super dives onto her bed and landed in a pile of pillows.

"One more thing to do," thought Shelly. She gathered her paper, scissors, markers and glue and got to work. She carefully drew a new skating charm for her sports crown. She had taken the first step to learning hockey!

I am Shelly Bean the Sports Queen!

Shelly Bean placed the crown on her head, stood tall in front of her mirror and thought, "I wonder what awesome sport I'll learn next?"

Tips for Learning to Ice Skate

Ice skaters should always use proper equipment such as elbow and kneepads and a helmet for protection.

1. Position Your Body:

Start on the ice with your feet shoulder-width apart and the blades of your skates facing the same direction.

2. Find Your Balance:

Extend your arms out to your sides about shoulder height like an airplane for balance.

3. Push and Glide:

Begin by pushing your right foot to the right and back on the ice. Keep your left leg bent and let your left foot glide forward. Continue pushing with your right foot and gliding on your left 10 times, slowly.

4. Switch Sides:

Now, push your left foot to the left and back on the ice. Keep your right leg bent and let your right foot glide forward. Continue pushing with your left foot and gliding on your right 10 times.

5. Check your body:

Start on the ice with your feet shoulder-width apart and the blades of your skates facing the same direction.

Ruff!

6. Switch One Skate at a Time:

Finally, try alternating feet by pushing your right foot to the right, then your left foot to the left and so on. Go slow!

Now you've got it!

Good posture is important for skating. Keep your eyes and chin up to see other ice skaters around you and remember to keep practicing and have fun!

Glossary

hockey stick: A long stick with a blade at the end used to move the puck across the ice.

puck: A round disk made of rubber that slides across the ice. Players must hit the puck into the goal net to score a point.

goal: A goal means two things in hockey:
1. The goal is the area where a player hits the puck to score a point.
2. A goal is scored when the puck crosses over the goal line and into the net.

slapshot: When a player is far away from the goal and hits the puck hard towards it by making a full swing with her stick.

offense: The team with control of the puck. They are trying to score a goal.

defense: The team without control of the puck. They are trying to stop the other team from scoring a goal.

faceoff: A faceoff happens at the start of a hockey game. The referee drops the puck on the ice between two players and they each try to hit it. A faceoff also happens after a timeout or after someone blows a whistle to stop play.

Safety Tips*

Ice-skating is a fun winter activity and also great exercise! The National Safety Council offers these tips to help you and your family enjoy safe skating.

- Wear skates that fit comfortably and provide enough ankle support to keep you on your feet.
- Have the blades professionally sharpened at the beginning of each season.
- Skate only on specially prepared skating areas where you are sure the ice is strong enough to withstand your weight.
- Always check for cracks, holes and other debris.
- Before setting out on your skating expedition, learn basic skating skills, such as how to stop and fall safely.
- Wear warm clothing and rest when you become tired or cold. Dressing in layers allows you to bundle up or cool down as needed.
- Never skate alone.

*Adapted from the National Safety Council

About the Author

Shelly Boyum-Breen grew up playing sports in her neighborhood with friends, her brothers and on her school teams. She found that the life-long benefits of sports for girls were so important that she needed to write this series and inspire girls across the world to play. Shelly resides in Minnesota with her spouse, has two adult daughters and continues to play sports and be active.

About the Illustrator

After designing books and working as a creative director in publishing, Marieka made the leap to become a children's book illustrator. Now with over 30 picture books in print, she loves creating artwork that engages and educates young readers. Marieka always aims to draw an environment where all children can see themselves, as well as the big wonderful world around them.

More action packed books in this Series:

- **Shelly Bean the Sports Queen Skates at the Hockey Rink**

- **Shelly Bean the Sports Queen Plays a Game of Catch**

- **Shelly Bean the Sports Queen Plays Basketball**

  And many more...